www.booksbyboxer.com

Published by
Books By Boxer, Leeds, LS13 4BS UK
Books by Boxer (EU), Dublin D02 P593 IRELAND
© Books By Boxer 2022
All Rights Reserved
MADE IN CHINA
ISBN: 9781909732766

No part of this publication may be reproduced or transmitted in any form or by any means, electronic or mechanical, including photocopying, recording or any information storage and retrieval system, or for the source of ideas without written permission from the publisher.

So you've received this book...

You must be notorious for your lack of spending (you certainly didn't buy this book yourself), and somebody you know thinks you're a tight git!

So sit down on your DFS sale sofa, grab a reheated cup of tea and flip through the pages. You might just learn a trick or two on saving cash the cheapskate's way!

(This book is recyclable - so rip it up and wipe your bottom once you're finished with it!)

PLATES TO PLENTY

Do you ever find yourself watering down your last dribble of washing up liquid, just so you don't have to open a new bottle? It's bad enough that your money is literally going down the drain, but now you're expected to add dish soap to your shopping list...

Take control of your cupboards and treat yourself to some gloriously cheap paper plates. You can spend less time washing your dirty crockery and more time watching your bank balance. Win, win!

ESTIMATED MONTHLY SAVINGS: £2/$2.50

DIRTY CASH

Dishwasher? More like all-in-one! You've already spent the cash on buying this legendary machine, but what if I told you that you can save your dosh by making it multi-purpose?!

Not only can your dishwasher wash other items (such as your shoes, laptop, and even your pet dog), but it can also double up as an oven for your food! Just be careful though - your tuna bake might get a little damp...

ESTIMATED MONTHLY SAVINGS: £20/$25

DUST MONEYS

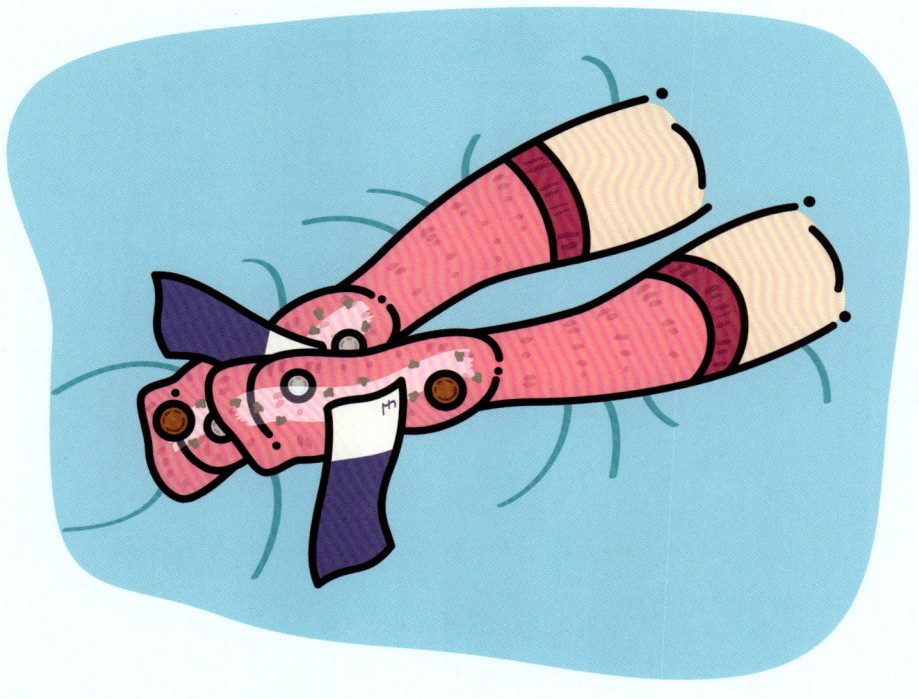

Got dust bunnies invading your floors but don't want to increase your weekly hoover costs? Turn your home from a dust-mite haven into a toe-tally spotless paradise with sticky tape!

Pop some double-sided sticky onto the bottom of your socks and waddle around your home like a lost penguin. Not only will you gather a load of dust, you might even find a lost penny or two!

ESTIMATED MONTHLY SAVINGS: £3.50/$4.50

UNDERWEAR - WIPEOVER

Socks looking a little holey? Pants seen better days? Don't chuck them away, they've got some life in them yet!

Why waste your precious pennies on cloths that end their life in your bin? Instead, take your old undies and socks and give them a new lease of life as a cleaning rag. Socks are amazing at clearing away dust, and your pants can be used to clean around your bathroom. (Maybe avoid using them to clean your kitchen though… nobody wants a knicker sandwich!)

ESTIMATED MONTHLY SAVINGS: £3/$4

COOKED FOR CASH

So you've just made yourself a lovely salmon dinner and notice the heat radiating from your oven. What should you do?

Well, why let that lovely, fishy-smelling heat go to waste? Instead of using the expensive tumble dryer, why not pop some freshly washed soggy socks and underwear onto a baking tray and let them bake for a little while? Yes, they might smell like fish, but your bank balance will thank you!

ESTIMATED MONTHLY SAVINGS: £10.50/$13

BRICK-A-BRACK HACK

Need some decorative storage space for your thrifted books? Maybe somewhere to keep your boxes of receipts saved over the last ten years? Don't go buying an expensive bookshelf or a set of drawers from the furniture shop, use your imagination and save yourself some money!

That skip in your neighbour's garden? It's full of cheap treasures from which you can build the storage of your dreams
(or nightmares…)

Some bricks and a plank of wood? Your new bookshelf. An old ladder? Towel rack. Wooden crate? Your brand new coffee table!

ESTIMATED MONTHLY SAVINGS: £100/$124

BUDGET BAGS

Do you spend your evenings doing fun things like watching teleshopping shows or reading leaflets? Why not use your time on more useful things, like chopping up your rubbish?

Cardboard boxes, juice bottles, and even food waste can be easily chopped up to save space in your bin – and by reducing your space, you can use the same black bag for longer! – What if it begins to smell, you ask? Well, spend your newly saved cash on some Freshbin powder!

ESTIMATED MONTHLY SAVINGS: 44p/50¢

BILLS ARE BANISHED

Radiators too expensive? Gas heater not taking the chill away? Don't waste your time and money on poor heating - get warm the old-fashioned way with a flickering, hot campfire!

Your living room will look much more homely with a roaring fire in the centre, and you can be assured that your house will be toastier than ever before! If it begins to burn out, then an odd chair leg or cupboard door will soon get it roaring again.

Don't forget a stick and marshmallows, you're in for a treat!

ESTIMATED MONTHLY SAVINGS: £80/$90

PICTURE IT

So you want to make your life seem more adventurous to those who visit your home. You work 9-5 and scrimp on your cash... we all know you haven't paid for a holiday in forever!

Google can make your life look glam with a click of a button! Just go onto Google Images, search for places like Benidorm or Turkey, and find a picture of a silhouette in a pretty place. Don't forget, it looks even more legit if it has writing across the image saying 'Stock' or 'Template'.

Print out 'your' new holiday pics and... voilà!

ESTIMATED MONTHLY SAVINGS: £800/$990

WIPED YOUR CARD

You buy massive newspapers just to read, then throw them away like they're worthless. Such a waste… don't you know you're killing trees?

Gone are the days of reading the back of air freshener cans - save the planet (and your pocket) by turning this old printed paper into your new trendy décor! Paste it onto the walls of your toilet, and then not only will you have an upgraded home, but you can complete Sudokus while you poop - and give your guests 5 minutes of entertainment too!

ESTIMATED MONTHLY SAVINGS: £5/$6

CLINK CLINK

So you've been to the pub with your mates and it cost you an arm and a leg. Don't let greedy pub owners take advantage of your boozy needs, make sure you bring home that fancy pint glass! I mean, you've already paid for it...

Now you don't need to buy a vase if you receive any flowers (we all know you won't buy any yourself), or you can pretend to have bought it as a heartfelt present and gift it to your favourite person!

Are you a Carlsberg or Budweiser type of vase collector?

ESTIMATED MONTHLY SAVINGS: £8/$10

SPARKLING SAVINGS

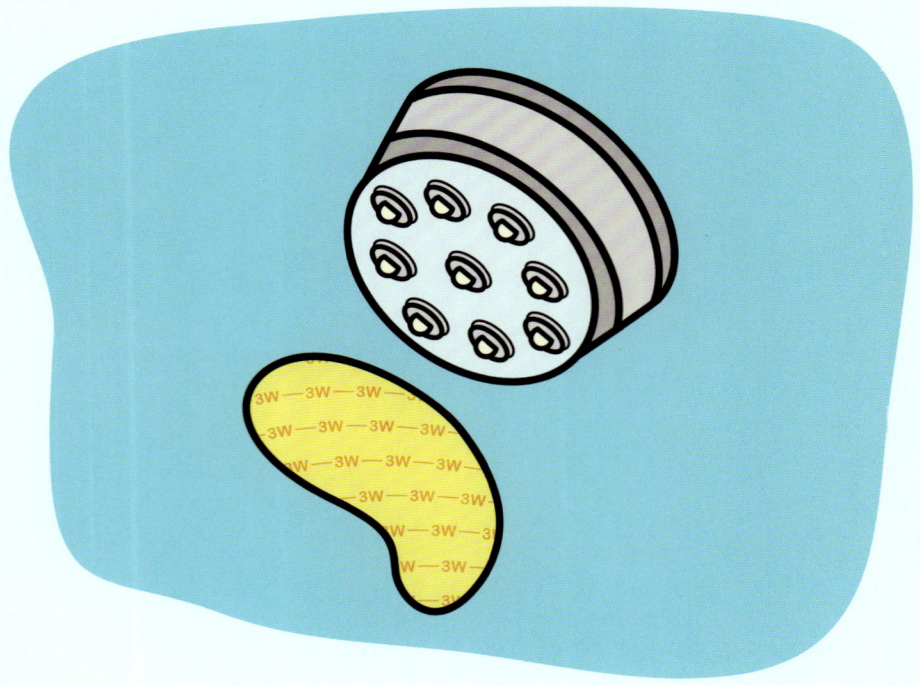

Take charge of your electricity charges and reduce your monthly light bill with this battery-operated hack!

You've seen those cute Christmas fairy lights, haven't you? Decorate your living space with masses of battery-powered light-up Santas, presents, and snowmen all year round, and you can save some pennies for the next holiday season!

ESTIMATED MONTHLY SAVINGS: £6/$7.50

TAP AND PAY

Did you know that you use approximately 150 litres of water every time you get a bath? That's around 28p per bath… outrageous!

It doesn't have to be like this though. If you have a family of four, you can save 84p just by using the same water. Just line your family up in dirt order, and make sure everyone has a dip in the bath before it gets cold. They might moan about bits of skin and hair floating around, but once they find out how much you're saving, you'll be considered a genius.

Top tip: If you get into the bath first, you won't notice a difference… but your family will!

ESTIMATED MONTHLY SAVINGS: £2/$2.50

PAN-LESS SPENDING

So you've taken your evening bath (and made your family use the same murky water), what now? You don't think that water's ready to go down the drain just yet, do you? NO! There's so much more life in this lukewarm liquid!

Grab your dirty pans and bring them into your bathroom! You can use your loofa to scrub off any tough bits of food, and the dead skin cells make a perfect grease remover!

(Who cares if your boiled eggs start tasting a little soapy?)

ESTIMATED MONTHLY SAVINGS: 60p/$1

$A \times Z = Y$

I HATE MATHS.

(But I LOVE counting cash!)

WEATHERED WALLET

The winter season is expensive. Heating on high, lights switched on at 4pm, and you need to replace those overused winter wellies. By the time spring comes along, your wallet has been wrung of cash!

Prolong the life of your beaten up boots with carrier bags! Yes, after being forced to pay 10p for a bit of plastic tat, you might as well put it to some good use! Simply wrap these bags around your chilly feet, and you can stop your socks from getting soggy on a rainy day.

ESTIMATED MONTHLY SAVINGS: £15/$18.50

WEAR IT OUT

Underwear is one of the most washed pieces of laundry ever! People wear them once and think it's dirty just because it has a few smudges here and there.

Well, why would you put on a load of washing if it's only knickers and socks? Get an extra day or so out of those stinky undergarments by turning them inside out. The sad truth is that it's very unlikely anyone is going to notice if your knickers are twisted (apart from the pong), so get saving!

ESTIMATED MONTHLY SAVINGS: £4.73/$6

X MARKS THE SPOT

So you want to be one of the cool kids on the block but don't want to part with your hard-earned cash. Who blames you? Spending more money on an item than it's worth, just because it has a tick on the side, really does seem pointless…

So, why aren't you DIY-ing your own branded outfits? If you can bear to part with £1 to buy a permanent marker, then you can save at least £40 on each posh bag or pair of shoes you were tempted to buy!

ESTIMATED MONTHLY SAVINGS: £120/$148.50

ANORAK ANO-RICH

Is bad weather making your savings a little soggy? You probably didn't intend for your rainy-day fund to be so literal... don't break the bank though, you can stay dry on a budget with bin bags!

One of the best inventions known to man, these black liners are perfect for many things - sledging in the snow, putting your rubbish in, keeping dust off suits, and even as a homemade witch costume! They have another use though... anoraks! Yes! These landfill loving tools make the perfect waterproof jacket when you don't want to splash the cash!

ESTIMATED MONTHLY SAVINGS: £10/$12.50

TOE-TALLY LOADED

Do your toes play peek-a-boo through holes in your cheesy, old socks? Stop playing whack-a-mole with your big toe and cover it up with this holey hack!

Keep a marker pen on you at all times, so when you spot a hole in your favourite socks you can colour it in quick to save pennies, and the embarrassment of showing your hairy toes to the world!

ESTIMATED MONTHLY SAVINGS: £5/$6

EYE ON THE PRICE

So, you rocked the NHS glasses look but accidentally sat on them. It's too late to send them to A&E, but with a little bit of TLC you can turn your smashed up glasses into some futuristic specs!

You're going to need some duct tape... pop out your lenses from your now destroyed frames, and place them over your eyes. Take your tape and stick them over your eyes (avoiding your brows – unless you want a free eyebrow wax).

Now you have the cheapest – and coolest – glasses in town!

ESTIMATED MONTHLY SAVINGS: £15/$18.50

GRANULATED SPENDS

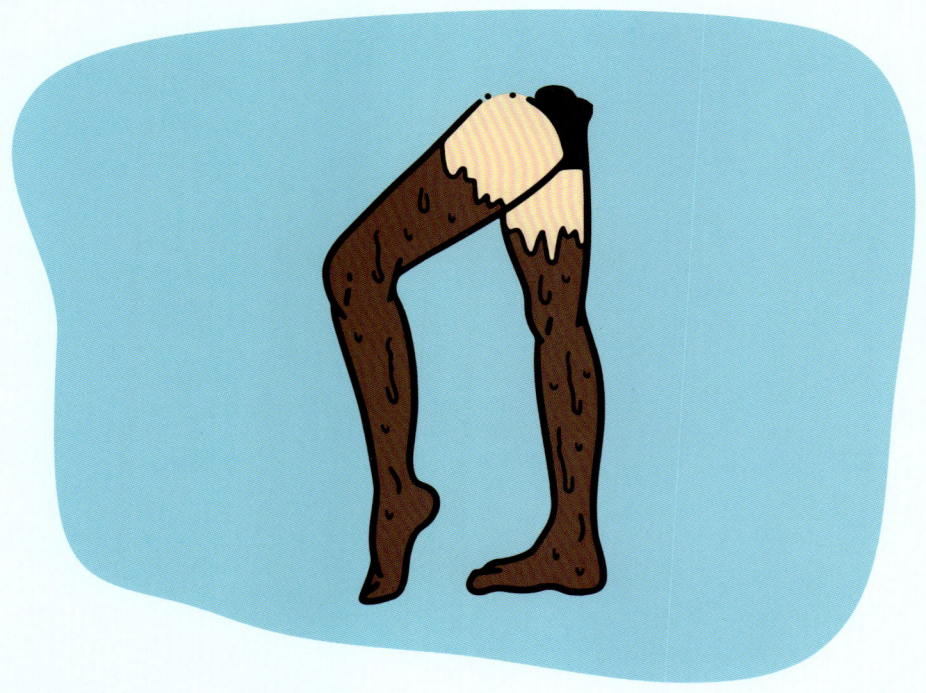

You want that sun-kissed glow, but tanning beds are a no-go and fake tan is patchier than your savings account… ditch the expensive brands and get yourself a jar of Bisto. Yes, you can add some gravy to your meat to go from looking like raw chicken to cooked beef… in onion gravy! If you become a religious gravy-tanner, you can save around £50 over the summer months!

So scrub those granules onto your legs and make sure you wash it off fully – otherwise you'll smell like a Sunday roast!

ESTIMATED MONTHLY SAVINGS: £10/$12.50

FASHIONably RATES

Don't feel like stretching your budget on brand new clothes every time you go through a hard breakup or dieting phase? Get yourself down the maternity isle!

Fashionable clothing with a little extra give to the waist, you can avoid those heart-breaking clothing clear-outs and save yourself from buying new jeans every two months!

ESTIMATED MONTHLY SAVINGS: £150/$185.50

HANDBAGS AND GLADRAGS

So, you think you're a fashion icon. You're nothing unless you're sporting the 2022 summer collection of 10p carrier bags. Aldi, Tesco, Heron foods… they're the top fashion brands to follow this summer. Ditch the Louis Vuitton clutch, Lidl's iconic colours really stand out alongside your F&F jeans and Pep&Co t-shirt!

These bags aren't just for your weekly shop. They're fashion accessories, and they're easily fixed if they rip. Have you ever stuck cello tape on a Gucci bag? Me neither.

ESTIMATED MONTHLY SAVINGS: £2,500/$3094

SHOE MUCH ROOM

Kids outgrow their shoes faster than you can say 'daylight robbery'. It's always one day before the school term starts when they decide to have a growth spurt, which means you have to dig into your pockets last minute to buy new.

Stop this hassle and buy their shoes 3 sizes bigger. "Too floppy" you say? Pad them out with socks, kitchen roll, or your kid's hamster. Whatever will keep them from whining about their feet - you know how much you'll save over the year.

ESTIMATED MONTHLY SAVINGS: £15/$18.50

VINTAGE FINDS

Your poor old granny has kicked the bucket and left her earthly belongings behind...

Take advantage of her old-fashioned style and nab those floral skirts and pleated pinafores before they're sent to charity! They might not be so popular right now, but everyone knows that 'vintage' clothes always come back into fashion eventually...

Just make sure they're not the clothes she passed away in, otherwise you'll have more to worry about, than just an itchy clothing tag!

ESTIMATED MONTHLY SAVINGS: £250/$309.50

LITTLE BUY BLUE

Are you sick of people complimenting the same two shirts over and over? You know it's because you're too tight to buy more fashionable items, but there is something you can do to soften the blow.

Buy blue! By buying a few identical blue t-shirts, nobody will know that you own more than one shirt, and the irritating compliments will stop. Don't forget – if you spill curry down one top, make sure to make an identical stain on the other top for authenticity!

ESTIMATED MONTHLY SAVINGS: £50/$62

TIGHT WEDDING

You've been invited to a wedding and the bride's chosen a beautifully detailed white dress for the occasion.

You don't want to buy a new outfit just to wear for one day, so why not wear one of your old dresses? Your prom dress is a little tight, but your wedding dress fits like a glove.

What better way to compliment the bride, than to wear matching attire!

ESTIMATED MONTHLY SAVINGS: £70/$86.50

LET IT RAIN

Is your coat smelling a little pongy lately? Don't waste your pennies by putting it in the washing machine, just wait for a rainy day and take a hike!

Your coat will smell wet and, well… wet, once nature does its thing, and it might even get rid of a few inconspicuous bits of dirt.

ESTIMATED MONTHLY SAVINGS: £5/$6

My wallet is like an onion, opening it makes me cry...

SOLAR SAVINGS

Is your house lit up like Blackpool Illuminations, and costing just as much? Let the big, hot star in the sky help in your bid to save cash!

Throw away those money-sucking bulbs and buy some cheap solar lights (who cares if they're meant for your garden), and decorate your home with butterflies, ladybirds, and mushrooms. You might need an abundance of lights and they might dim down after a few hours, but the sun will surely charge them up for some extra hours of light, ready for another indoor lightshow!

ESTIMATED MONTHLY SAVINGS: £6/$7.50

PARDON MY PENNIES

[Cash saving intensifies]

So you want to watch a film. Don't ruin your movie night because of the cost of energy, pop your TV on mute!

Even better, you don't need to lose out on the movie experience, just change your TV settings to include subtitles and you can be assured not to lose the plot!

Bonus: your date for the evening will absolutely love the fact that you keep a tight hand over your wallet.

ESTIMATED MONTHLY SAVINGS: 1p/1¢

SNIPPET SAVINGS

Part 1 of 73
00,000, 000 views • 00 Month 0000

0 000CHANNEL

Think you're a bit tech-savvy? Put your knowledge of computers to good use with this mega savings hack!

The cinema costs a lot of money. You pay for the seats, movie, and snacks, and come out with an overdraft. But you don't have to go through all this hassle to watch a new movie. You can be guaranteed that there will be snippets of every part of the movie online. Get them downloaded and saved in chronological order.

Now you're ready to hit play 55 times!

ESTIMATED MONTHLY SAVINGS: £15/$18.50

PENNY-PALS

Let's face it, the way you're (not) spending means your social life is at an all-time low. But don't let that stop you.

Try to limit yourself to one phone call a day. When you're not using your mobile, switch it off and pop it away. By doing this, you're saving almost half a penny every time you would have otherwise charged up your phone. - £1.09 a year!

ESTIMATED MONTHLY SAVINGS: 9p/11¢

iCASH

We're definitely not phone-ist here. But it's the 21st century and you're walking around with a Nokia 6110... get your act together! Maybe you don't want to splash the cash on upgrading to an Android or Cr-apple, but at least make it seem like you belong in this era.

Take a marker pen and draw something that resembles an apple on the back of your beloved retro phone. At least now you can fool a few people into believing you have the new Apple iPhone 27...

ESTIMATED MONTHLY SAVINGS: £25/$31

TRIAL FOR A WHILE

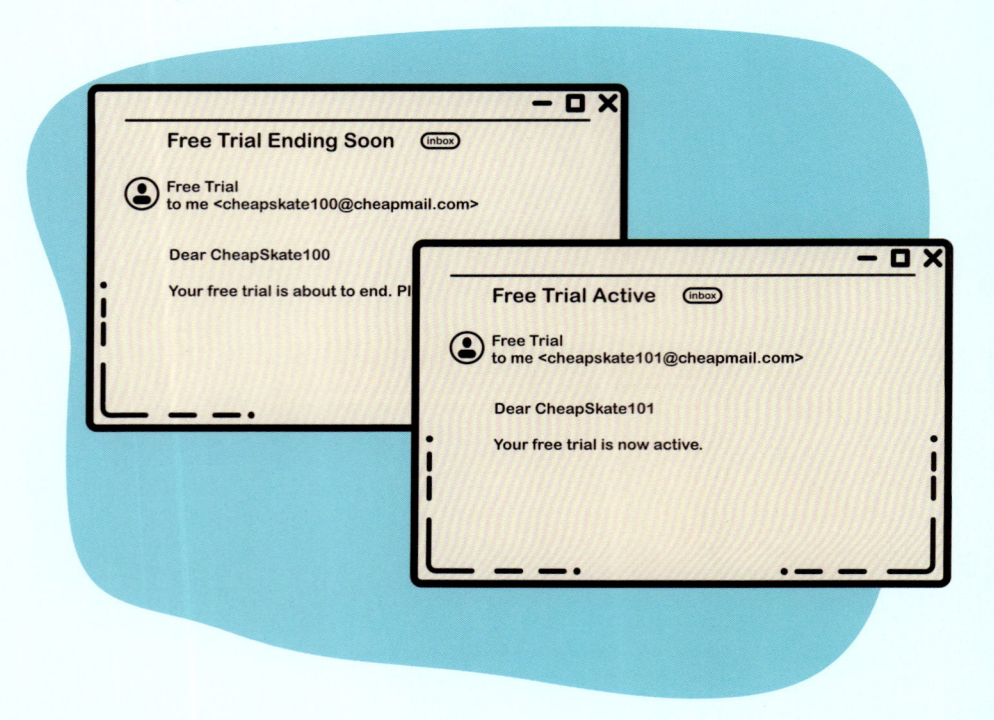

Free Trial Ending Soon (inbox)

Free Trial
to me <cheapskate100@cheapmail.com>

Dear CheapSkate100
Your free trial is about to end. Pl...

Free Trial Active (inbox)

Free Trial
to me <cheapskate101@cheapmail.com>

Dear CheapSkate101
Your free trial is now active.

You don't want to give greedy businesses your hard earned cash but still want to reap the benefits of owning a Prime account or finding your long lost cousins. We get it.

There's a reason free trials are so popular, but why stop at only one trial run? Every time your trial is about to end, cancel it (so you don't get charged), and create a brand new email! You can stream the entire TV series without spending a penny, and nobody is going to question the '123funkyflappypenguins6969!!@msn.com' email you just created.

ESTIMATED MONTHLY SAVINGS: £7/$8.50

THE WAILS ON THE BUS

Don't waste your mobile's battery charge by listening to your favourite tunes while travelling on a public bus... use your initiative and sit next to someone who's wearing earphones.

Nine times out of ten, a person wearing earphones will have their music on max, so choose a victim and put your ear against theirs to enjoy a fresh new playlist, absolutely free!

ESTIMATED MONTHLY SAVINGS: £0.09/11¢

SURE SALE

You like a bargain, but did you know you don't need to wait until items get reduced? Take a tech shop for example... you can wait for that expensive laptop to go on sale, or you can scratch the casing and bust one of the USB ports – you could even pocket a few of the keyboard buttons beforehand. You're bound to get at least 20% off the RRP!

ESTIMATED MONTHLY SAVINGS: 20% or more off your chosen item.

WIRELESS TRANSACTIONS

You know you're a cheapskate when all your friends have wireless earphones and you're still walking around like it's 2007, with wires sticking out of your phone. The joke's on them though, because you're going to get some modern earphones for no extra cost! Those old chunky earbuds of yours can lose the wires... simply snip them off for wireless (and music-less) earphones, and show off your brand new Airpods!

And if you feel the need to add a charging case to the mix, an old mint tin is sure to do the trick!

ESTIMATED MONTHLY SAVINGS: £100+/$124+

PENDING PAYMENTS

You've received your Amazon order and, although they're not damaged or anything, the items you've bought haven't filled that black hole in your soul. Do you think your money is lost on that extra-large carrot plush or complete N-Dubz discography?

Don't give up hope just yet! Amazon can only take their trusty delivery staff's word that these items were delivered… just drop a 1 star review with a comment like "This item would be brilliant – if I actually received it!!", and sure enough, you'll either be offered a refund or get another heat-activated llama mug sent to your door!

ESTIMATED MONTHLY SAVINGS: how ever much you spend online.

ON THE CLOCK

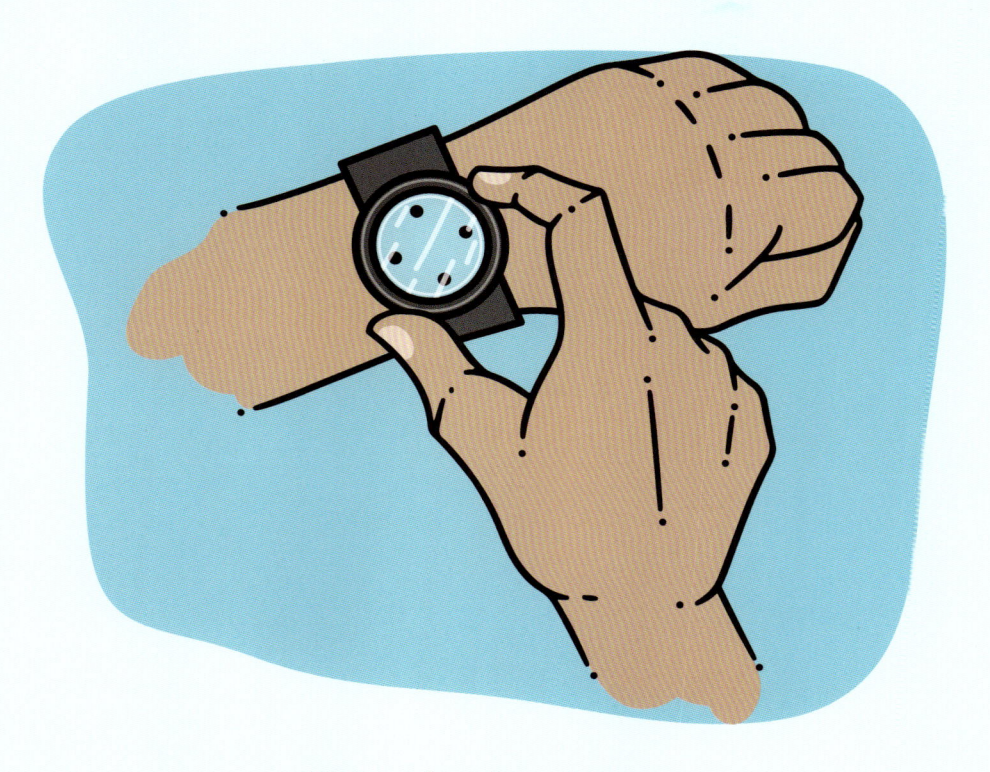

Tick, tock, tick, tock… stop.

Your handy watch has stopped. How on earth are you going to tell the time now? You're sure not going to fork out a few quid for batteries…

You have two options: You can keep it on your wrist for decoration and ask every stranger you walk past for the time, or you can count 'one Mississippi, two Mississippi' and move the seconds hand as you go…

ESTIMATED MONTHLY SAVINGS: £2.50/$3

SPENDING SPUDS

Your phone is dead. Your tight self doesn't want to spend money to get it charged and working again, but you've got no choice.

Or do you? A farmer's best friend, potatoes are great for baking, mashing, or chopping into chips, but they also conduct electricity! Yes - spuds might be the way to fix your cheap ways. All you need is a potato and a phone charger... Stick the charger into the tattie and your phone, and watch how it (very) slowly but surely fills up your battery!

ESTIMATED MONTHLY SAVINGS: 9p/11¢

RE-WIRE MY FIRE

Did you know that most old telephones can be used even during a power-cut? Due to being run on separate cables, it's potentially possible to rewire your home so your mobile can be charged for free!

What do you mean you're not a trained electrician... would you rather pay for a professional? I didn't think so...

ESTIMATED MONTHLY SAVINGS: 9p/11¢

ROUTING FOR YOU

Are you so tight that you can't even fathom forking out for a good wireless connection? As long as you live next to somebody younger than 45, you're in luck!

You can guarantee that anyone between the ages of 18 and 30 will have a quirky wifi name with a password that matches (something along the lines of 'BT phone home'). Though if your neighbour is 30 or over, you might have to become friends with them and peak at their modem when they're not looking – the password will be something like 'FSH32345jkFJFFJ2143'

ESTIMATED MONTHLY SAVINGS: £28/$35

The best way to save money?
Forget who **YOU** borrowed it from!

FOOD & DRINK

GET IT WHILE IT'S HOT

Fancy yourself a steaming hot cup of tea, but don't fancy your electric bill going up? Limit the brew boil to once a day!

Get yourself a nice big flask (don't worry, you'll save more money in the long run), and fill it up in the morning, so you can have a cheap, tin-tasting cuppa with your reduced value sandwich!

ESTIMATED MONTHLY SAVINGS: £4/$5

MILKING THE MONEY

Milk in cereal. What purpose does it have? It makes your cereal float around till it goes all soggy, then stays in your bowl till after you've finished eating. What a waste of perfectly good milk.

Floating crumbs and slight oaty taste aside, this excess milk is perfectly fine and can be used for other milk containing things – tea, coffee, mac and cheese... the possibilities are endless!

ESTIMATED MONTHLY SAVINGS: £3/$4

DOUBLE DIPPER

Hooked on tea but don't want to dip into your bank account? Pour yourself a cuppa – this hack is going to boil your brains!

When you make your first cup of tea, take out the teabag before pouring your milk. If you pop it into a fresh cup, you can use it for another brew round later! Granted, the second cup of tea might taste like stale water, but using teabags more than once isn't against the law. Highly frowned upon, yes… but after learning that you can save approximately 75 teabags a month, you should be beyond caring by now!

ESTIMATED MONTHLY SAVINGS: £2/$2.50

SALTY SAVINGS

How many times have you gone into a fast food restaurant and noticed an abundance of sachets, just hanging out on a condiment station… Shake up your monthly spending and remove salt and pepper off your shopping list by collecting sachets! You can then top up your shakers, at no extra cost!

You don't think anyone keeps a tally of the sachets do you?

ESTIMATED MONTHLY SAVINGS: £2/$2.50

BREAK THE BANK

Sick of your guests eating all your biscuits? How dare they? They came out of your pocket, not theirs!

Fool them into thinking there's more by cutting them in half! They will either get put off by thinking somebody (you) has tampered with them, or they will feel full in half the time! You can save on average 2 packs of biscuits a month! A win - win situation really...

ESTIMATED MONTHLY SAVINGS: £2.50/$3

COLD HARD CASH

You're seriously going to buy ice? Literal bags of frozen water? Are you crazy?!

Put it back and find your freezer… you have a whole box full of ice to your disposal! That ice on the edge, the one that makes it hard to open and close the door sometimes? Chip some off and add it to your drink, and you'll feel nice and refreshed knowing you didn't spend a quid on cubed water.

ESTIMATED MONTHLY SAVINGS: £1/$1.50

MAMA MIA MONEY

HALF IT

How do people go about their lives knowing they're wasting perfectly good pasta water by pouring it down the drain? Despicable!

You can use pasta water for many things – to wash your floors, water your plants and even to pop in the coffee machine for your morning brew! Like a fine Italian wine, your coffee will bring an essence of ravioli romance to your life.

You'll be Don Macaroni of the cheapskate's Mafia!

ESTIMATED MONTHLY SAVINGS: 25p/31¢

CHOMP YOUR CHANGE

So you're chomping on your last piece of gum, and don't want to buy anymore just yet. Not only does it cost you money to buy more, but people hover like vultures as soon as they see the shiny wrapper and smell the minty fresh fragrance…

You're not going to swallow it so why not save your gum till later? Yes, it might be a bit tough to chew at first, and it might not taste quite as fresh, but that's nothing a little drop of toothpaste can't handle.

ESTIMATED MONTHLY SAVINGS: £2.40/$3

WATERLOGGED WALLET

If you're as cheap as we are, you'll have watered down pasta sauce once or twice to make it go further. Don't think it has to stop at sauces though... why not try this handy hack with other things, like beer or vodka!

If you don't mind your beer being a bit bland, or curdling your Baileys, then you can save yourself some pennies (and drunken texts to your ex) by adding some water to the mix. This funky cocktail might drop your alcohol volume a bit, but who wants to get bladdered anyway?

ESTIMATED MONTHLY SAVINGS: £20/$25

MOULDY MONEY

Fancy a cheese sandwich but your bread, cheese, and butter are all growing alien specimens? Don't grab your shopping bag just yet, these essential items still have life in them!

Your cheese will only be mouldy on the outside, so chop away at its edges till there's no blue, green or white in sight! Your butter should be fine if you scrape the top off, but if not, let it melt a little and stir it in (it'll build your immune system). Bread will be a little trickier, but if you cut out the big bits of mould, it should be fine for at least another day...

ESTIMATED MONTHLY SAVINGS: £5/$6

CRUMBY WALLET

You're feeling a little creative and want to try your hand at baking. Great! Time to bring out your ingredients! No... you don't need to spend a fortune to make something remotely edible.

You see that biscuit tin? It has months upon months of crumbs – perfect for a cheesecake! With a mix of butter, you can turn those obscure stale crumbs into your next masterpiece – for less money!

ESTIMATED MONTHLY SAVINGS: £2/$2.50

BEAN THERE, DONE THAT

You settle down to eat your chips and find you're out of tomato ketchup once again! Now your chips taste like disappointment and potato. What a shame...

Don't throw that bottle just yet though, you can make your very own budget ketchup using... you guessed it! BEANS! Next time you open a tin of beans, run them through a sieve so you can collect that tasty juice without any pesky beans ruining the party. I bet you can't taste the difference, much...

ESTIMATED MONTHLY SAVINGS: £1.50/$2

POUR THE PENNIES

Don't waste your wage on bottled water... all water comes from the same place – the sky!

Put some open containers into your garden when the clouds are looking a little dark, and when it rains you will have yourself a collection of cold, fresh rainwater to keep you hydrated on the go!

ESTIMATED MONTHLY SAVINGS: 64p/$1

BON APPÉTIT

Want to treat your special someone to a grand feast? Why not opt for a fancy French dinner, on a budget!

Go into your garden to catch your main course – snails! Perfect for a classic Escargot dish! Make sure you double up on the garlic though, just to disguise the potentially earthy taste…

ESTIMATED MONTHLY SAVINGS: £5.50/$7

CANINE CASH

So your tea break is getting a bit too expensive… those digestives aren't as cheap as they used to be.

Fear not! If you've got a pet dog, you're in luck! You know what goes perfect with a hot cup of tea? Gravy bones. These crunchy snacks are enriched with vitamins and are great for keeping your canine teeth clean and healthy!

If it's good enough for your pooch, it's good enough for your afternoon tea.

ESTIMATED MONTHLY SAVINGS: £4/$5

Money talks... But all mine ever says is goodbye!

HEALTH

B.O.G.O.F

Wiping your backside has never been more expensive. These boring little paper squares are used once before getting flushed down the bog, never to be seen again…

What a waste! A fun, cheaper alternative to toilet roll is newspaper! You can read the news, complete a Sudoku and ponder over your horoscopes while you go number two, then wipe your bottom and go! It might be a little stiff at first, but the pros definitely outweigh the cons… just be careful of papercuts!

ESTIMATED MONTHLY SAVINGS: £4/$5

FRESH FIVERS

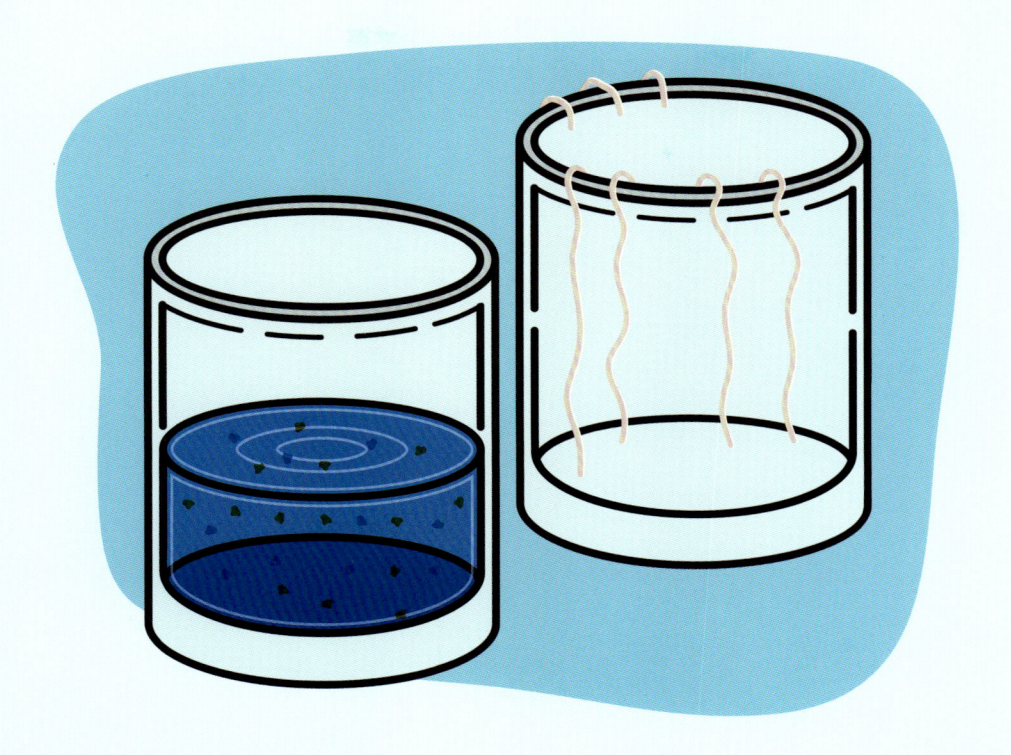

Do you find yourself spending a fortune on mouthwash and floss just to get that minty fresh feeling?

Cut down on your spends by reusing your dental products. Your floss should last you 2-3 goes, so long as you wipe the plaque from it, and your mouthwash can be easily spat into a beaker, ready to use the following day!

It's only disgusting if you share it with others...

ESTIMATED MONTHLY SAVINGS: £3.50/$4.50

MONEY LAUNDERING

Many expensive factors go into washing your clothes: running the washing machine and tumble dryer, using detergent and fabric softener… even using water and electricity. Why is it so expensive to stay clean?

It doesn't have to be. Save time and money doing your laundry by showering with your clothes on! You can smell like your favourite shower gel all the time, and you'll have extra money to spend on more important things like deodorant!

ESTIMATED MONTHLY SAVINGS: £13.40/$16.50

SOGGY SAVINGS

Only people who like to flaunt their cash sing "Rain, rain, go away"… but we cheap folk know better than that. Rainwater is an asset. It's free and wet, which means you can use it for many different things.

Why not take a rainwater bath? Though a little cold, it'll do the same job as tap water, and might even bring some spiritual enlightenment to you (or just make you a bit soggy).

ESTIMATED MONTHLY SAVINGS: £5/$6

MMM, FRUITY!

You're cheap, but you're not 'smelling like a skunk's armpit' cheap. We cheapskates like to smell fresh and sweet too, but the cost of perfume is extortionate… Who's going to pay so much for everyone else's smelly convenience?

This is where your 5 a day comes into play. Pick your favourite fruit, peel it, and rub it all over your body (then eat it). Be careful though, you'll be extra sticky and might attract wasps rather than a hot suitor!

ESTIMATED MONTHLY SAVINGS: £45/$55.50

GRATER SHAVINGS

Professional pedicures costing an arm and a foot? Don't worry, you can make a splash without spending hard-earned cash with this great tip (toe)!

You don't need to buy expensive foot spas when you already own a foot sized bowl… yes! Your kitchen is full of amazing tools that are perfect for treating your toes. Fill up your washing up bowl with water, and find your trusty cheese grater to use in place of a Ped Egg (just don't forget to wash it before grating your parmesan afterwards…).

ESTIMATED MONTHLY SAVINGS: £15/$18.50

TOOTH FAIRY FUNDS

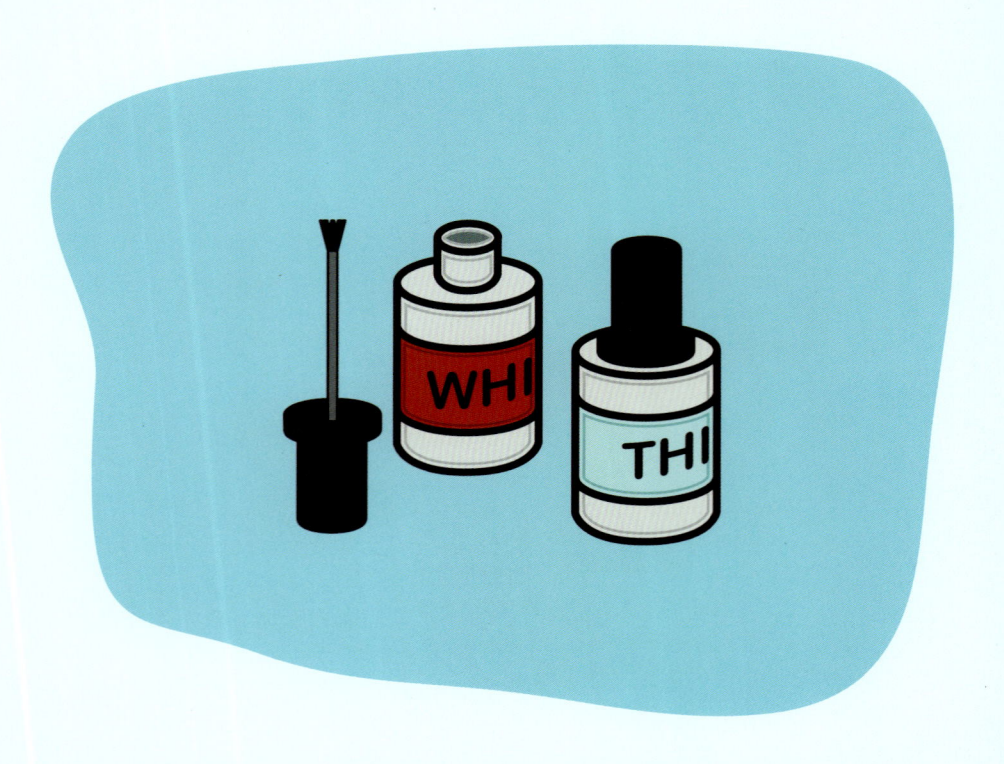

So your teeth are starting to look a bit yellow. Your dentist has proposed a 'deep clean', meaning they want you to dig deep into your pockets and clean them out, spending cash on unnecessary procedures.

Why not DIY your dentistry and give yourself a glimmering smile with Tipp-Ex! Yes, this office supply is perfect for giving you toothpaste advert-worthy teeth! If all else fails, knock out all your teeth and put them under the pillow for some fairy funds!

ESTIMATED MONTHLY SAVINGS: £95/$117.50

ESCALATED FUNDS

You want to get a beach bod before the summer but YouTube fitness videos just aren't working. Don't succumb to buying a treadmill, just go to your local supermarket and run up the escalator for the ultimate fitness hack! – Bonus, it's free!

P.S. This only works if the escalator is heading downwards, and there's a slight possibility you might be taken away by the men in white coats...

ESTIMATED MONTHLY SAVINGS: £250/$309.50

SKINNY STRIPS

Everyone has hair they don't want anymore, but some of us don't want to pay the extra cost just because we look like a hairy yeti. Don't let your rogue hair ruin your cheap plans, buy some duct tape!

Strong enough to hold together the universe (and Ikea furniture), duct tape is the perfect example of beauty maintenance on a budget. Who needs these fancy moisturising wax strips, when you can wrap yourself up in tape and acquire perfectly hairless (and skinless) legs!

ESTIMATED MONTHLY SAVINGS: £10/$12.50

EVERY LITTLE HELPS

Drop the price of every plop with this unique money-saving hack!

It's perfectly fine for dog owners to use doggie bags on their pets, but why are humans so different? You've probably acquired many 10p carrier bags over the year, so get them used! Simply open a bag and place it into the toilet, pop down your lid and there you go! A flush-less toilet system!

Tip: You might want to throw the bag outside afterwards – it might get a little whiffy!

ESTIMATED MONTHLY SAVINGS: £2.70/$3.50

SHAKE YOUR CHANGE

So you want to get fit. Everyone knows protein shakes are a fitness freak's best friend, but the cost of whey powder is enough to turn you towards burgers!

Instead of losing pennies on whey powder, lose the pounds by blending up your own fitness shake! All you need is some grass from the garden, a few leaves and a dash of sugar and you can be on your way to becoming a health influencer – or to throw your guts up…

ESTIMATED MONTHLY SAVINGS: £34/$42

COST CUTTER

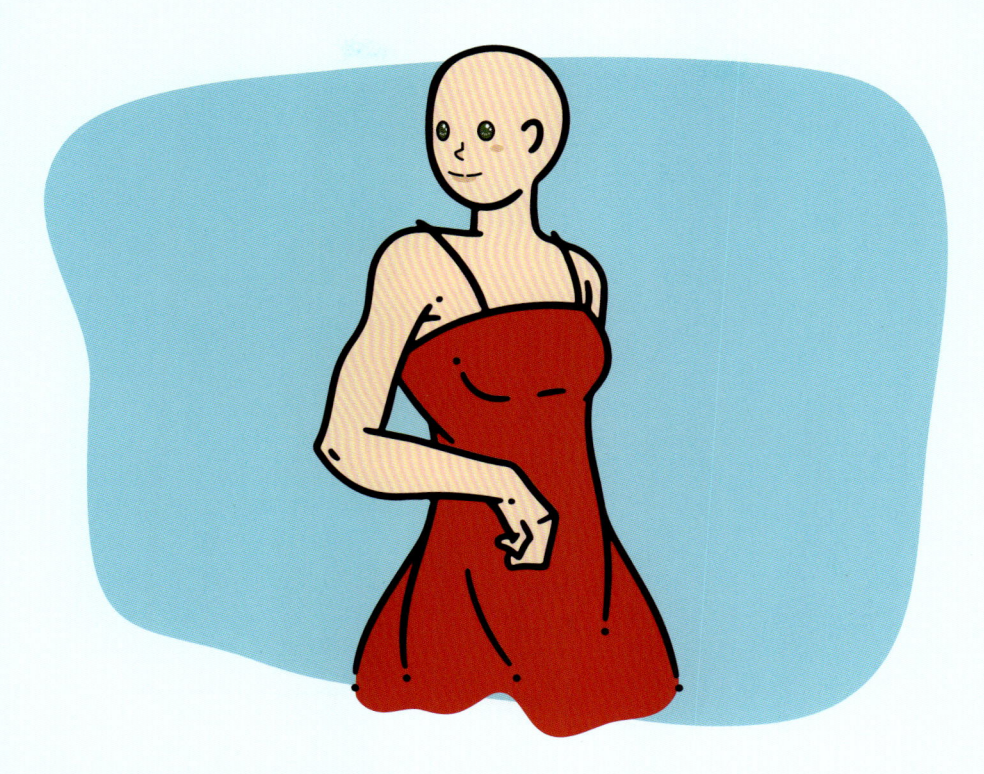

Shave a little on your weekly shop by crossing shampoo and conditioner off your list. All you need to do is take a shaver to your head and you can save around £72 a year by not washing your hair! You might need to invest in a shaver to keep your head smooth and hairless, but the small spend will prove profitable in around four months.

You'll even save yourself from buying hair products, accessories and styling tools – what a win!

ESTIMATED MONTHLY SAVINGS: £6/$7.50

FOUNDATION OF FUNDS

Foundation is expensive and tricky to figure out. The colour, consistency, and cost all play a part in the quality of your face.

Who needs Estée Lauder and Dior when you can have B&Q beauty? At £1 for a paint tester pot, you can save so much money and still look like a painted maiden. Just find your skin tone among the swatch cards!

ESTIMATED MONTHLY SAVINGS: £35/$43.50

TAKE A BROW

So you want to tattoo on your eyebrows.

If your cheap self is seriously considering spending over £200 on micro blading your face, then you should relook at your options.

A permanent marker costs all but £1 and hurts much less than being stabbed in the upper eye 1000 times… Oh, and if you have a change of heart, you can scrub it off (eventually!).

ESTIMATED MONTHLY SAVINGS: £200/$247.50

I wanted to make pasta, but I was penne-less!

TRAVEL

BUDGET BRUM

Cars are just expensive tin boxes with wheels. You have to pay taxes and insurance costs, fix them up when they break, and it all adds up while your petrol gage goes down!

Though there's not much you can do about yearly taxes and MOTs, there is a way you can limit your petrol usage while still taking your car for a spin. If you're planning on a road trip, the hilly scenic route is the way to go. Simply switch off your car at the top of every hill, sit back and let your car drive itself down. After all, there's no point wasting precious petrol when you have gravity on your side!

ESTIMATED MONTHLY SAVINGS: £25/$31

HOLIDAY SPENDS

So you were finally persuaded to let go of some cash and now you're off to Turkey (the land of knock off brands!), but getting there is going to be a bit of an issue, since you won't want to pay to take your clothes with you.

The baggage charges are crazy, airlines charging so much so you can take a fresh pair of underwear and your bright green speedos... why not just layer up? I'm sure you can handle sitting for 5 hours dressed in 10 layers of clothing – especially when it won't cost you a penny!

ESTIMATED MONTHLY SAVINGS: £20-£50/$25-$62

SPLASH NO CASH

Cars are very greedy when it comes to screen wash. In the summer, it takes 3 attempts to wipe away splattered insects then another 5 attempts to wash away the streaks.

Why wash away your cash every time a seagull poops on your windscreen? Recycling is the in thing, baby! Try reusing your washing up or mop bucket water… you can save on your water usage and provide a soggy leftover snack for those pesky bugs!

ESTIMATED MONTHLY SAVINGS: £1/$1

DEFLATED CASH

Why is it always at the most inconvenient time when our vehicles decide to play up? You don't want to spend any more cash than necessary to keep your car running, but then you run over something sharp and your tyre begins to deflate – just like your savings…

Don't worry though! You don't need to race down to the nearest garage for a new tyre, just dig out some playdough, mush it into any distinct holes, and you can be on your way.

ESTIMATED MONTHLY SAVINGS: £65/$80.50

STICKER FOR MONEY

Your MOT is due, and that means one thing: MONEY. Your exhaust is extortionate, your steering is steep and your door alarm is daylight robbery at its finest. All this could have been covered up except for one cog in the works... the check engine light.

Like a halo around your wallet, this little light tells the mechanic that something isn't quite right. They might need to drain your oil... or your bank account. Not to worry! By sticking a sticker over the light, you can disguise your misfortune and leave your issues for another year – it's totally not obvious...

ESTIMATED MONTHLY SAVINGS: £200+/$247.50+

SCENIC SPENDS

It's a beautiful day! The sun is shining, not a cloud in the sky and you fancy a long, chilled out, scenic road trip... only problem is, your petrol costs more than your kidney!

Not to worry though, a day rider ticket for the bus is only a couple of quid, and will get you from A to B, and every stop on the way! Just press the stop button every time you want to look at a cow, Tesco Express or some roadkill, and pack yourself a sandwich for lunch too!

ESTIMATED MONTHLY SAVINGS: £50/$62

TICKETS PLEASE!

MEN

So you've snuck onto the train without paying to save yourself a couple of quid, but you've just heard the dreaded "Tickets please!"... what should you do?

You could sit and wait in your seat, pleading your innocence and end up paying a hefty fine, or you could run to the nearest toilet like you've just eaten a vindaloo... What's it going to be? I doubt any conductor is going to force a diarrhoea-induced victim to show their ticket... just make sure you make the sound effects for authenticity!

ESTIMATED MONTHLY SAVINGS: £20/$25

ON YOUR TIKE

You don't want to look like a caveman… what's the big deal? There were no cars in the stone age and people traded using small rocks and bones. They lived a simple, cheap life.

Nowadays, you have to pay for transport. You can't just hop on the nearest mammoth's back and ride to the flashiest cave house. Don't go spending your hard earned cash on a cheap Honda Civic, just 'borrow' your nephew's Little Tike's car (you know the one), and Fred Flintstone your way through town!

ESTIMATED MONTHLY SAVINGS: £1,500/ $1856.50

SQUEEZED FOR CASH

Are flights becoming far too expensive for your cheapskate self to afford? You still want to go abroad with your mates though...

One easy route you can take is to contort your body to fit into their suitcase. At £15 an hour, contortion classes will be worth it if you like to go on your jollies at least once a year. After all, the flight is only 8 hours...

ESTIMATED MONTHLY SAVINGS: £500/$619

PEDAL THOSE POUNDS

Do you want more money? Have you noticed that your bike has two whole wheels? Well, you're in luck!

Why not sell one of those pretty bicycle wheels and turn your trusty pedal bike into a unicycle? Not only will you gain a little extra cash, you'll also make your friends extremely jealous of your brand new circus act... all you need now are some juggling balls!

ESTIMATED MONTHLY SAVINGS: £45/$56

ECO-FUNDS

So you're a tight git who wants to save the earth. Congratulations, Greta Thunberg is sure to like you!

You've bought a brand new electric car to save the earth, and your bank account from the price of petrol, but even electricity is burning a hole in your pocket... Why not invest in solar panels? Not only will you recharge your vehicle with no effort or extra cost, you'll also look like an eco-conscious earthling!

ESTIMATED MONTHLY SAVINGS: £120 /$148.50

PENSION PUSHER

The price of bus passes have gone up drastically over the years, and now you need a bank loan every time you step foot on one... not to worry! Your dear old granny is sure to let you use her bus pass (or not notice if you nab it...).

All you need to do is draw yourself some wrinkles, perm your hair and wear your Sunday best, and you're sure to get on the bus for free!

P.S. Make sure you sit at the front to make it more realistic.

ESTIMATED MONTHLY SAVINGS: £75/$93

SCHOOL'S OUT

Hopping on the school bus for discounted prices was the height of our childhoods. It's a shame we had to grow up and use public busses to go places...

So you want to get to the supermarket next to the local high school... Just wait at the bus stop till you see the school bus, and hitch a ride! Who cares if you're 32 next week, dig out your old school blazer, because you're going on a journey you'll never forget! Don't forget, only the cool kids sit at the back...

ESTIMATED MONTHLY SAVINGS: £40/$49.50

I bought a cheap thesaurus today.
Not only is it terrible,
it's terrible.

SOCIAL

SAVE THE DATE

It's your mother's birthday. You love her dearly and she deserves all the happiness in the world, but paying 99p for a bit of sparkly card is outrageous!

Don't worry though, you can create your very own personalised birthday card on a Microsoft Word document and print it out on cheap paper. A pre-used bill envelope is the perfect way to gift your card – just fold it in half if it doesn't fit. Your mum will absolutely love your creativity!

ESTIMATED MONTHLY SAVINGS: £1/$1

COSTA-LOT

So your good friend has invited you to Costa-lot for an expensive cup of coffee... The beauty is, expensive places like this always have a point system. Save so many points and you get 1 item free!

You know you won't come here often, so why not guilt your friend into giving up their points? Of course, your cheap soul needs them far more than they do, and they wouldn't want to deprive you of a nice, hot, FREE coffee, would they?

ESTIMATED MONTHLY SAVINGS: £2.30/$3

SPLIT THE BILL

You and your friends go out for a catch-up meal. Some posh Italian place where the prices are high and the menu is alien to you… Don't worry!

Order as much as you can handle, and even if you can't eat it all, you can ask the waiter for a 'doggy bag'…

When it comes to paying, why not suggest doing it in a fair way – splitting the bill! I'm sure your friends won't mind that your food came to £45 and theirs was a measly £10 each…

ESTIMATED MONTHLY SAVINGS: £20/$25

RE-GIFTED

Did you get mountains of bath sets at Christmas? We all know you won't waste enough water to use those bath bombs... so why not wrap them up for a less cheap friend to enjoy?

As long as you remove all distinctive gift tags and gift it to someone other than the person who gave you it, you should be fine to do this for every occasion. Who knew having friends could be so cheap?!

ESTIMATED MONTHLY SAVINGS: £7.50/$9.50

GATECRASHING CASH

You heard from your cousin that Aunt Denise is making carbonara tonight… your favourite!

You're overdue a visit to her house anyway, so why not go at, let's say… 5pm? You know she can't resist feeding her family, so make sure you go there on an empty stomach, and don't forget to stay for dessert too!

ESTIMATED MONTHLY SAVINGS: £10/$12.50

CHEAP CELEBRATIONS

You received some beautiful birthday cards this year, and it would be a real shame to just throw them away…

Instead of watching them go to the rubbish dump, why not recycle them and send them on to celebrate another birthday? All you need to do is cross out the names and rewrite them… Of course if you want it to look a little more professional, you could always invest in a bottle of Tipp-Ex (as long as it doesn't break the bank, that is).

ESTIMATED MONTHLY SAVINGS: £2/$2.50

BANK OF MUM AND DAD

Walking, packing, spending money... don't put yourself through the hardship of going shopping, just take a visit to your parent's house!

You know your mum can't deny you your favourite turkey dinosaurs and tinned beans, and your dad really wants you to try this new spicy Pot Noodle... They know you only go to raid their cupboards, but they love your visits and occasional grunts as responses!

ESTIMATED MONTHLY SAVINGS: £150/$186

BARGAIN BOOZE

Your friends have dragged you to the pub and insist on getting you bladdered, but all you really care about is not spending so much per drink! God forbid they begin doing rounds…

Ask the bar staff for a glass of free tap water, and whenever you take a sip of your pint, top it up with a bit of water. Your pint becomes endless, and your evening is the cheapest on record!

ESTIMATED MONTHLY SAVINGS: £15/$18.50

GRAVELY CHEAP

Want to show your girlfriend how much you love her, but don't love her enough to splash out on some fresh flowers? Why not take a trip to your local graveyard? Full of freshly placed flowers, this patch of holy land is your very own florist shop! – Keep an eye out for a dead person with the same name, you might be able to pick up a personalised plaque or ornament too...

ESTIMATED MONTHLY SAVINGS: £20/$25

CONFETTI WITH CHANGE

Here comes the bride, all dressed in white…

You're too cheap to buy heart shaped confetti, so why not rip up last month's gas and electricity bills? I'm sure the happy couple's wedding photos will look amazing, with scrappy bits of paper with ineligible words floating above their heads…

Who said weddings had to break the bank?

ESTIMATED MONTHLY SAVINGS: £1.50/$2

CHIN CHIN

So your friends have blackmailed you into stepping foot into your local pub… the land of milking money out of your pockets for 'fun'. It's all well and good when your friends pay for your drinks, but taking it in turns with rounds? Now that's going too far.

Don't sit around waiting your turn to pay for every man and his dog, excuse yourself to go to the toilet, and sneak out through the window to ensure a cheap return to your home.

ESTIMATED MONTHLY SAVINGS: £15/$18.50

BIG DAY SMALL SPENDS

Congrats! You're getting hitched! This means your life savings will be found in a ditch and you'll be living off tinned beans for seven months! Not to worry though, here's a tip to make your big day as cheap as possible.

You want to invite all 3 friends, your mum and your second cousin twice removed… Don't waste your precious pennies on fancy card invitations, just rip up some blank space on your old bills, and send them in reused tax-due envelopes! – So exquisite!

ESTIMATED MONTHLY SAVINGS: £22/$27

BORROW BUDDIES

You get paid at the beginning of the month and by the time you're on day 10, you're skint! There's no use being friends with those who are in the same predicament, find yourself some mid-month wage buddies to hang out with! Now you can go drinking in week 3 of the month, without worrying about buying some reduced bread!

(Even better are the 'friends' who get paid weekly... a bank-loan on legs!)

ESTIMATED MONTHLY SAVINGS: £100/$124

PLOPPED OUT

You've spilled your curry all down yourself while eating your Wednesday night takeaway treat, but you don't want to invest in stain removal powder to fix your ways...

Not to worry, just take a visit to your friend's house... They'll definitely believe that a seagull pooped all down your front while you were walking up their driveway... a madras loving seagull, that is!

ESTIMATED MONTHLY SAVINGS: £2.50/$3

Teach kids to drive.
They'll never have enough money for drugs.

WORK

PLUG IN POCKET

So your desk is nicely positioned next to the plug in the wall. Ideal!

If you haven't already taken the initiative to plug in your phone, now's the time to charge! It's free, and there's only a 45% chance your boss will be annoyed about it. Just blame it on recurring power cuts, and not your inability to part with your cash.

ESTIMATED MONTHLY SAVINGS: 9p/11¢

SINK OR SWIM

Your sink is full of grimy dishes, your pipes are blocked, and you really don't want to splash the cash on hiring a plumber... Why not just bag up your mucky dishes and wash them at work?

Sure, you might get some funny looks as you walk around with everything but the kitchen sink in your bag (it's not the 3 week old lasagne smell drawing the attention)... but you will save on washing up liquid, water and the need for a plumber. Win, win!

ESTIMATED MONTHLY SAVINGS: £30/$37

HIGH CARD FLUSH

A heated bathroom, freshly cleaned toilet, free loo roll… it's no wonder so many people poop on company time! Get your act together and start now. Save on water and toilet roll by clenching your butt-cheeks till you get to work – you'll even get paid for it!

ESTIMATED MONTHLY SAVINGS: £2.50/$3

CHILLED CASH

What's the point in having a fridge anyway? You spend money to buy things to put into it, and spend more money keeping those things cold. What a waste.

Unplug the refrigerator and take your chilled goods to work. There's a perfectly free fridge there, so claim the bottom shelf and keep your groceries fresh!

(Don't forget to label it, or it'll become Colin's afternoon snack!)

ESTIMATED MONTHLY SAVINGS: £3.10/$4

BREW-TIFUL

It's a cold evening and you're about to leave work. The weather calls for a nice hot brew, but that means using your own teabags.

Stop. Why not bring your flask into work, so you can make yourself an evening's worth of tea on a budget? – Don't forget your hot water bottle too!

ESTIMATED MONTHLY SAVINGS: £4/$5

PRINT THE MINT

So you've just insured your car (what a heartbreak!), and now you're wanting to print out the 102 page fine print document you were sent. Don't waste the ink in your brand new printer, use your work's resources to fulfil your printing needs!

102 pieces of paper, 4 ink cartridges and a ton of electricity, all saved by using your brain!

ESTIMATED MONTHLY SAVINGS: £2/$2.50

SOLELESS

So you sit at your desk all day, clicking buttons and stapling papers to earn a bit of cash... what's the point in ruining your brand new shoes? Preserve your soles by taking your shoes off in the office!

Your colleagues won't mind if the area around your desk smells like BO and cheese... after all, once they know how much money you're going to save, they'll be joining you in this barefooted presentation!

ESTIMATED MONTHLY SAVINGS: £10/$12.50

STAY STATIONARY

The office is like Aladdin's cave... drawer upon drawer of unused pens, paperclips and elastic bands. You know your workmates won't miss a pack of staples or an envelope if they suddenly go missing...

Don't dig deep into your pockets for stationary, fill them up! Like a sweet shop for 30 year olds, you know you can't do without those shiny gold paper fasteners and fluffy sellotape!

ESTIMATED MONTHLY SAVINGS: £3.50/$4.50

DOWN IT!

You're recommended to drink 6 pints of water a day. 6! Who do these health advisors think they are? Demanding you drink... they don't pay your water bill!

Don't waste precious tap water on your health and wellbeing... go to work and find your nearest watercooler... you'll look like the fittest person in the building as you down cup after cup of stagnant water (it's only been there 3 weeks)...

ESTIMATED MONTHLY SAVINGS: 60p/$1

TELL THE TOOTH

Your work has so many free facilities, and the bathroom sink is one of them! I don't think there's a 'bring your toothbrush to work day', but there should be, and you should do it every day.

Imagine the amount of time and water you'll save just by brushing your tooshies at work... even better if you're running late!

ESTIMATED MONTHLY SAVINGS: 25p/31¢

MEALS ON WHEELS

So you work 9-5 and by 4:30pm you're starving! Why use your home electricity to ease your rumbling belly, when your workplace has a perfectly good microwave!

Simply bring your dinner into work in the morning, and heat it up before you go. This way, you can eat your hot cottage pie on the bus home. Full belly and cheap electricity bill for you!

ESTIMATED MONTHLY SAVINGS: 1p/1¢

ES-SPOON-AGE

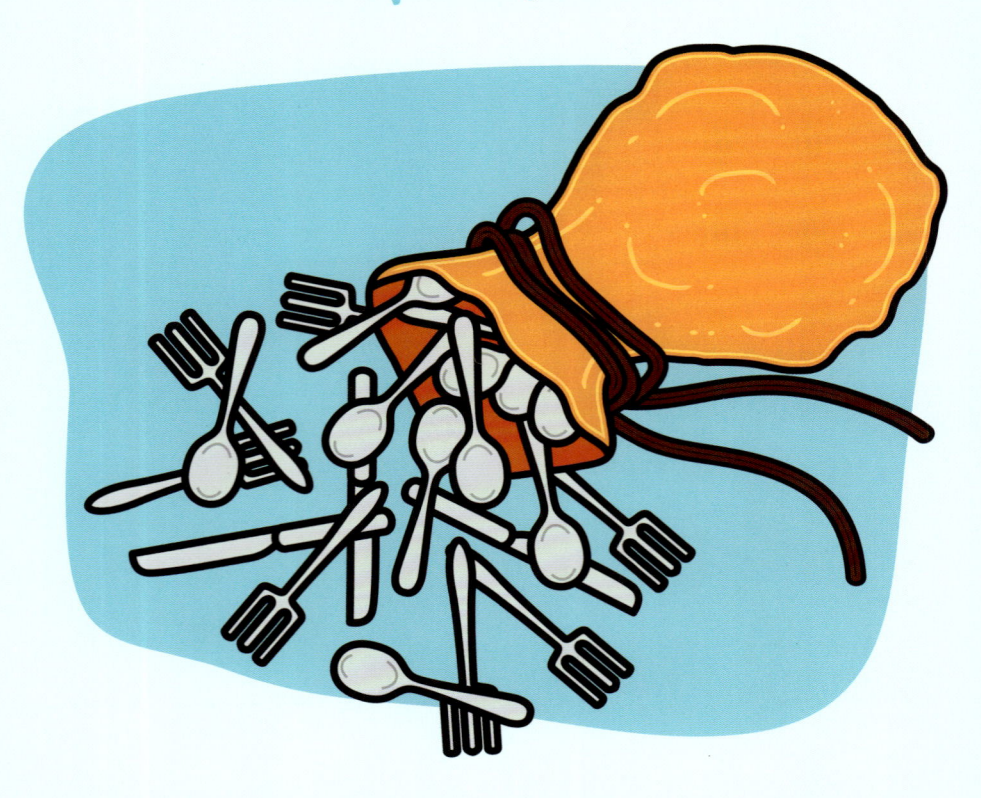

Work drawers full of cutlery? Want to earn some easy money? Become the spoon thief of your workplace, and work your way to riches!

There's nothing wrong with 'borrowing' cutlery from the work's canteen, but what if you 'accidentally' forget to give it back, and did the same thing every week for a full year? Now you have an abundance of shiny knives, forks and spoons! – Perfect for selling as scrap metal, you might land yourself with a bit of cash!

ESTIMATED MONTHLY SAVINGS: 10p/12¢

PREMIUM PRICES

You have some important business to discuss on the phone, but you know you'll be on hold for 2 hours, and the call costs £3.60 per minute... you're not seriously going to pay out of your own pocket, are you?

Call the number from your work phone! Your boss will love you forever (and it's not like you were told not to call premium rated numbers...).

ESTIMATED MONTHLY SAVINGS: £3.60/$4.50

NET-FLEX

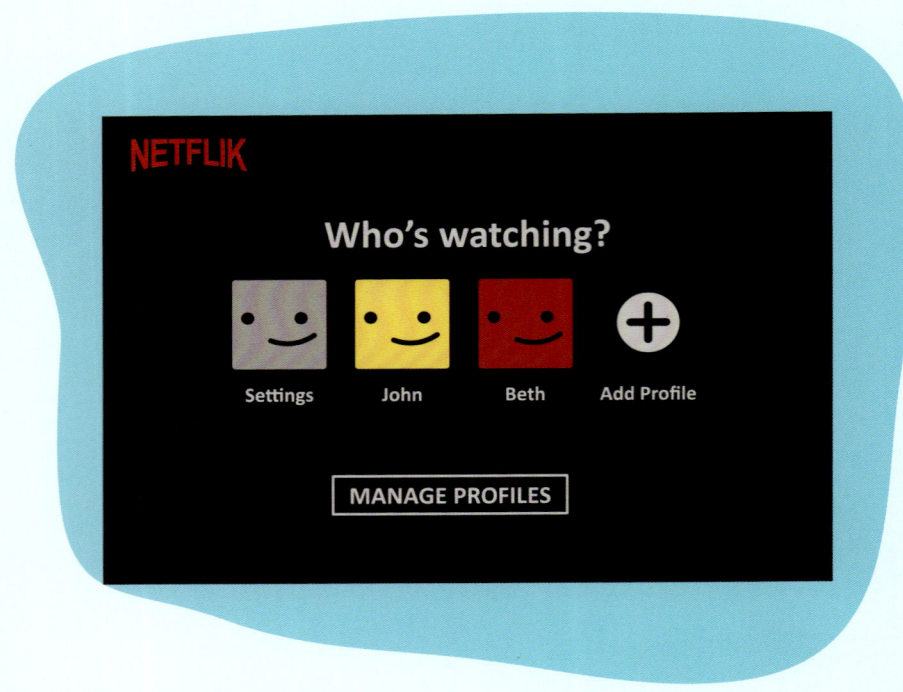

Who's watching?

Settings | John | Beth | Add Profile

MANAGE PROFILES

So you broke up with your annoying ex, but it just so happens you still have their Netflix account. Don't stop watching your favourite shows, use this to your advantage!

They don't need to know you're still logged in, just change your name to 'Settings' and set yourself a lovely picture of a cog and you'll be able to fool them for months!

ESTIMATED MONTHLY SAVINGS: £6/$7.50

books by BOXER